THIS

COLORIGBOOK

BELONG TO

UNICORN

FASHION

I LOVE UNICORN

BELIEVE IN MAGIC

I BELIEVE IN UNICORNS

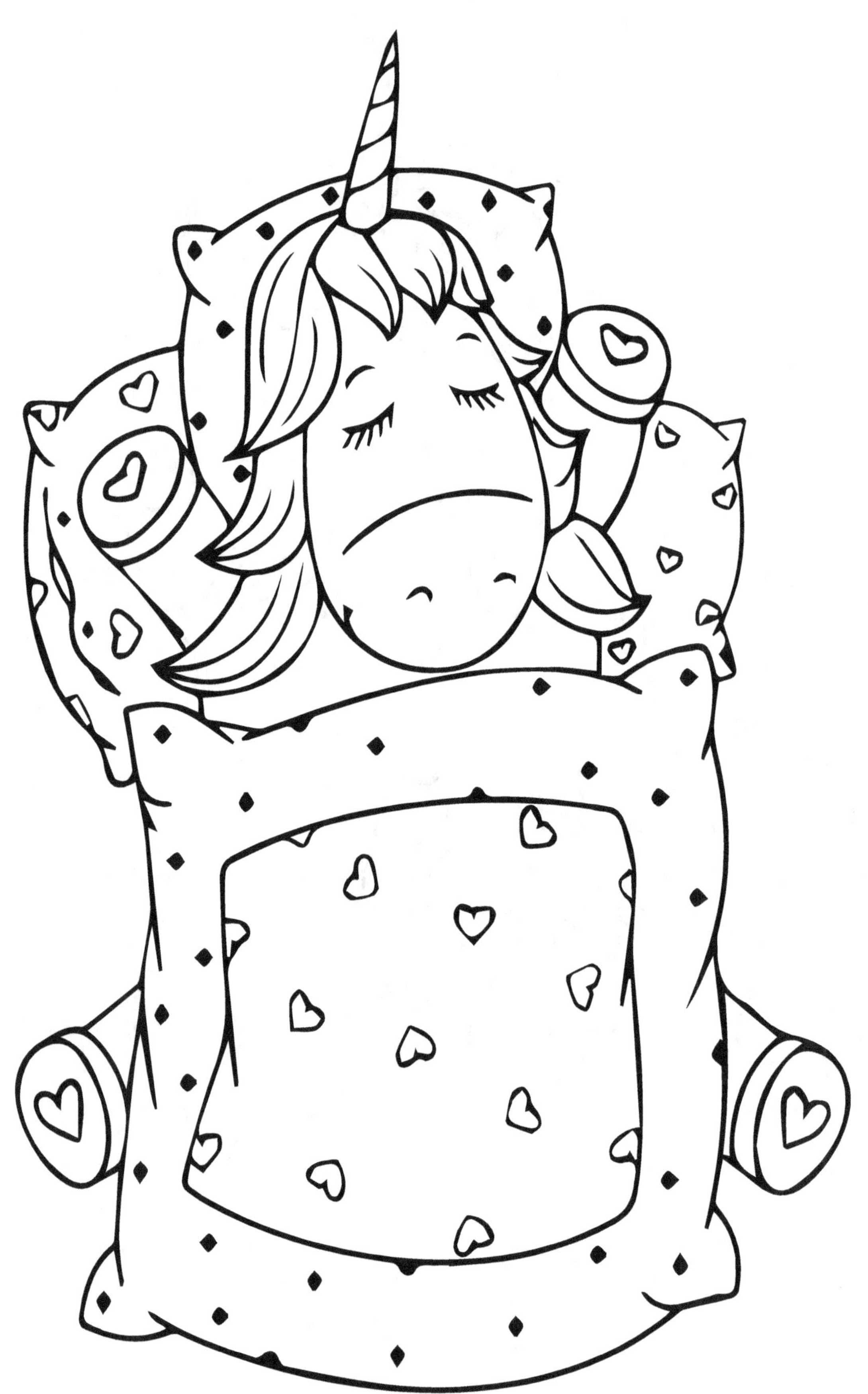

Unicorn

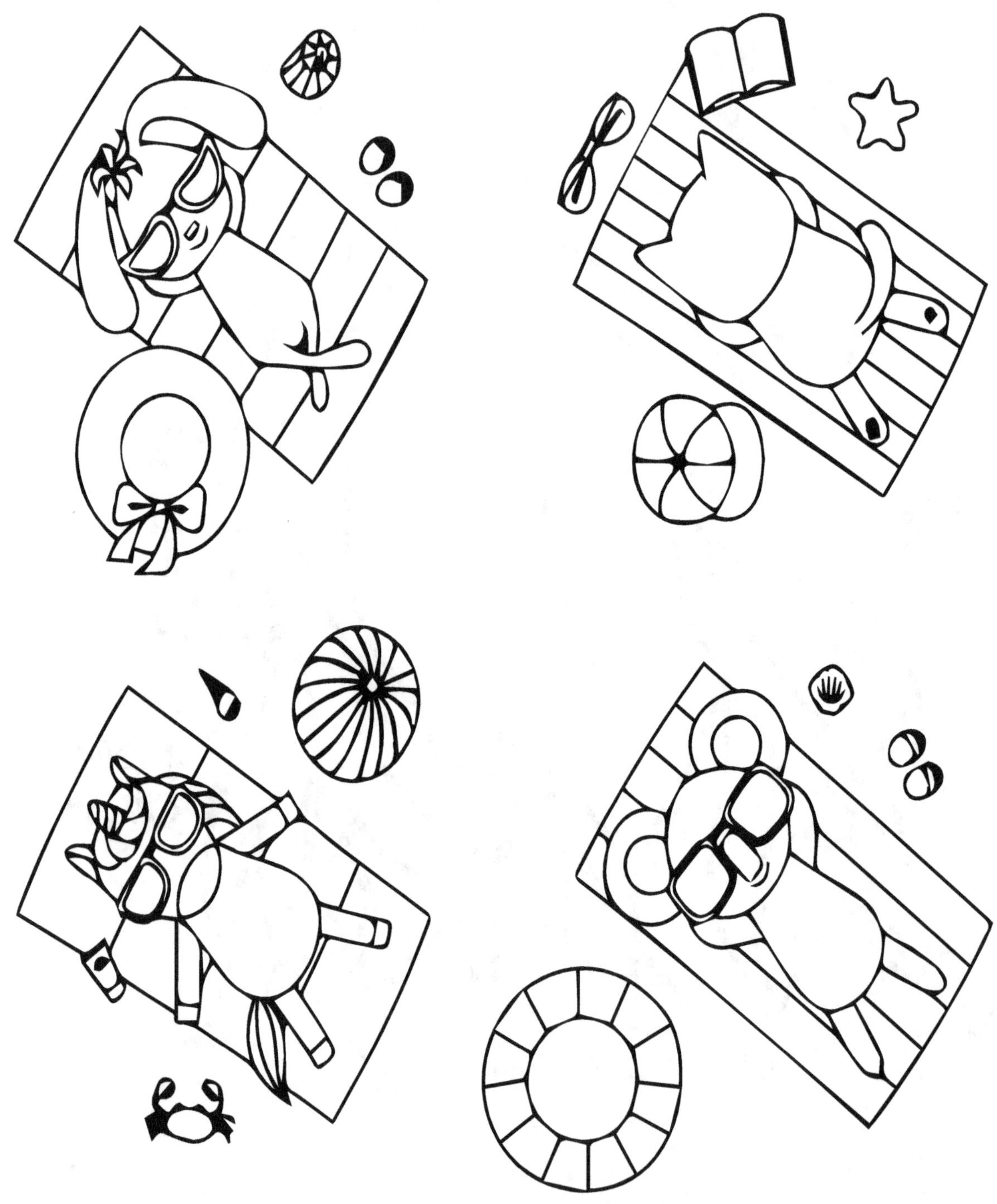

Let's
DANCE!

I BELIEVE IN UNICORNS

Unicorn

www.ingramcontent.com/pod-product-compliance
Lightning Source LLC
Chambersburg PA
CBHW081746250726
48657CB00010B/3424